NATIONAL PARKS
JOURNAL FOR KIDS

THIS
JOURNAL
BELONGS TO

_____

NATIONAL ★ PARKS ★ JOURNAL
FOR KIDS

Log and Remember Your Awesome Outdoor Adventures

JASON AND ABBY EPPERSON

ROCKRIDGE PRESS

This book is dedicated to our national park
adventurers, Jack, Ethan, and Henry.

First Rockridge Press trade paperback edition 2022

Rockridge Press and the Rockridge Press logo are trademarks or registered trademarks
of Callisto Media Inc. and/or its affiliates in the United States and other countries and may
not be used without written permission.

For general information on our other products and services, please contact our Customer
Care Department within the United States at (866) 744-2665, or outside
the United States at (510) 253-0500.

Paperback ISBN: 978-1-68539-447-9

Manufactured in the United States of America

Interior and Cover Designer: Alan Carr
Art Producer: Sue Bischofberger
Editor: Jeanann Pannasch
Production Editor: Melissa Edeburn
Production Manager: Lanore Colopriso

Illustration © 2022 Patrick Corrigan, cover and pp. v, vi, 22, 44, 66, and 88; all other
illustrations used under license from shutterstock.com.

10 9 8 7 6 5 4 3 2 1 0

WELCOME TO YOUR ADVENTURE

National parks are some of the most awesome places on Earth. Their landscapes, plants, and animals are so special that we have federal laws to protect them. Best of all, they are open to everyone to explore!

In this journal, you'll get to write about your travels to four parks. You will also get to draw, play fun games like seek-and-find, and complete fill-in stories. Feel free to use this journal by yourself or with a partner and be sure to ask for help if you need it.

It's important to keep national parks just as they are. "Take nothing but pictures, leave nothing but footprints" is a common expression among outdoor adventurers. When you're in a national park, follow all park rules, and always ask your adult before going anywhere.

Most important—have fun!

You'll want to begin your journal before you leave for your trip. So, let's get started!

★ TRIP ★

ONE

(Name of the national park you are visiting)

OFF TO THE PARK!

It's time to start tracking your adventure to a national park!

Date I'm leaving: _____

Who I'm going with: _____

Where I'm staying: _____

I'll be there for _____ **_hours   days   weeks_**
                    number   _(circle one)_

What I'm packing: _____

_____

_____

_____

What I wish I could pack: _____

_____

_____

_____

WHAT I KNOW ABOUT THIS NATIONAL PARK

This park is in the state of _____

It is near the city of _____

This park is known for _____

_____

This park should have: *(check all that apply)*

☐ A campground

☐ Mountains

☐ A river

☐ A lake

☐ Sand

☐ Snow

☐ Trails

☐ Trees

☐ Beaches

☐ Tours

☐ Caves

☐ Flowers

☐ Beautiful views of:

  ○ water

  ○ trees

  ○ open land

MY PLANS

The thing I'm most excited to do is: _____

_____

_____

The thing I can't wait to see is: _____

_____

_____

One thing I'm curious about is: _____

_____

_____

I hope the weather is: _____

_____

I hope the park has: _____

_____

_____

I hope I don't forget to: _____

_____

ARE WE THERE YET?

I'm traveling by: 🚗 ✈️ 🚆 🚲 ⛴️

The coolest thing I've seen out my window is:

_____

The weirdest thing I've seen out my window is:

_____

Travel snacks and meals I've had: _____

_____

Travel snacks and meals I've spilled: _____

_____

I am traveling _____ miles.

This **will   will not** be my first time at this park.
    (circle one)

The funniest thing that's happened so far is:

_____

_____

_____

WE'RE HERE!

Ah, we finally arrived.

(circle a bold word in each sentence)

My first impression was:
WOWZA! **It's okay.** **Yawn.**

It took **less more** time to get here than I expected.

As soon as we got here, I **ate slept explored unpacked**.

The first person I met was: _____

_____

Place your next steps in order from 1 to 5:

_____ Map out a hike

_____ Watch park film or talk to ranger

_____ Check weather forecast

_____ Fill water bottle

_____ Locate nearest bathroom

THE SOUNDS OF NATURE

Sound is a big part of nature. At the park, you'll hear people's voices, phones, and cars. Animals find and warn each other with sounds. Wind and water make sounds, too.

Sit somewhere away from crowds. Close your eyes for one minute and listen.

What do you hear?

_____

_____

_____

_____

_____

_____

_____

_____

_____

THE PARK SO FAR

Things I've done so far: *(check all that apply)*

☐ Talked to a ranger

☐ Taken a picture at park entrance sign

☐ Went on a hike

☐ Walked through a museum

☐ Seen or heard an animal

☐ Had a snack or picnic

☐ Went on a scenic drive

☐ Had to put on a warmer jacket

☐ Got in the water

☐ Had fun!

I think this park is: *(check all that apply)*

☐ Big

☐ Small

☐ Quiet

☐ Loud

☐ Wild

☐ Historic

☐ Exciting

☐ Pretty

☐ A place I'd like to visit again

☐ Other _____

ANIMAL FEATURES

What helps an animal survive in this park?

(check all that apply)

☐ Wings   ☐ Scales

☐ Claws   ☐ Feathers

☐ Teeth   ☐ Fur

☐ Gills   ☐ Other _____

If you could be any animal in this park, which

would you be? _____

Why? _____

_____

_____

_____

_____

_____

_____

BE A PLANT DETECTIVE!

The rangers need you to help them observe plants in the park! Look for clues to help the plants survive.

Plant: _____

Where sighted: _____

Color: _____

Smell: _____

Have you ever seen it before? **Yes No**

I thought it was: **beautiful ugly weird boring cool**

Its overall plant shape looks like this:

GETTING TO KNOW THE NATIONAL PARKS

Did you know there are more than sixty national parks in the United States? Let's learn some fun facts about some of them!

* A painter named **George Catlin** was the first to think of the national park idea. He was worried that people would hurt the landscape by building on it as America grew.

* **Yellowstone** is the world's first national park. It became a national park on March 1, 1872.

* The hot water that bubbles up from the ground in **Hot Springs National Park** in Arkansas is thought to be able to heal people. This park is in the Zig-Zag Mountains, named for the way they look from above.

* More than 600 cliff dwellings can still be found at **Mesa Verde National Park**. These dwellings give us a line to the past by showing us the work of the Indigenous peoples of the American Southwest.

THE BIG PICTURE

Draw your favorite feature of the park.

SEEK AND FIND

Try to find these things in and around the park:

- ☐ A few people taking the same picture
- ☐ Any animal you've never seen before
- ☐ Baby in a stroller
- ☐ Bicycle
- ☐ Bones
- ☐ Cliff
- ☐ Dog on leash
- ☐ Fence
- ☐ Fish
- ☐ Giant (as in *huge*!) rock
- ☐ Gift shop
- ☐ Information kiosk
- ☐ Lizard or snake
- ☐ "National Park Service" logo
- ☐ Park ranger
- ☐ People on a picnic
- ☐ Recycle bin
- ☐ Red car
- ☐ Restroom
- ☐ River/stream
- ☐ Someone laughing
- ☐ Trail map
- ☐ Tree shorter than you
- ☐ Tree taller than you
- ☐ Warning sign
- ☐ "You are here" sign

The most unexpected thing I saw was:

_____

A WACKY LUNCH

Ask a fellow traveler to help fill in the blanks.

_____ was _____ through the
person　　　　　*action ending in -ing*

_____ with their _____ kids in _____
natural place　　　　　　　*number*　　　　　*noun*

National Park, when they came across a very

_____ tree. "Look," they said to their kids,
description

it's the _____ tree in the world.
　　　　description ending in -est

_____ asked a ranger for directions to a _
same person

_____ area, and _____ down
type of place　　　　　　*action with -ed*

with their kids for lunch. They all had peanut

butter and _____ sandwiches, carrots, __
　　　　　food

_____slices, and _____ chips. Their favorite
food　　　　　　　*food*

part of the meal was their _____'s
　　　　　　　　family member

homemade _____ _____ _____.
　　　　　scent　　*color*　　*food*

When they finished eating, they _____
　　　　　　　　　　　　　action with -ed

their trash and headed to the _____ trail for a
　　　　　　　　　　noun

_____.
description

WISH YOU WERE HERE

Write a postcard to a friend or family member at home. What have you seen that you want to tell them about?

MAP A TRAIL

Map a trail you hiked or design a trail of your own! Draw the shape of your trail, and use the map key to mark the things you might see. Add your own sights to the key.

Trail name: _____

Day and time hiked: _____

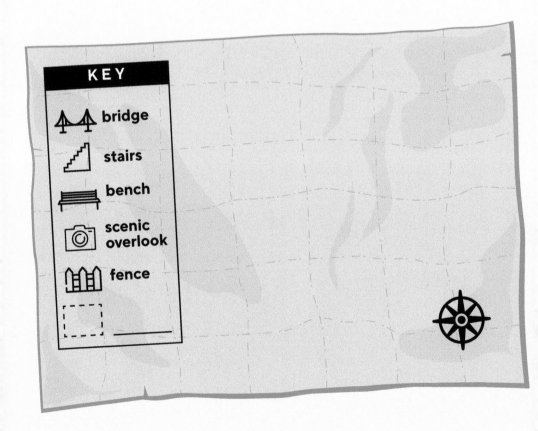

KEY

- bridge
- stairs
- bench
- scenic overlook
- fence

OBSERVE
YOUR SURROUNDINGS

Fill this out when you get to a special place, such as a trailhead or a scenic overlook.

Location: _____

The ground feels _____.
(Examples: hard, rough, smooth, grassy, wet)

The air feels _____.
(Examples: cold, sticky, breezy, warm, still)

When I look around, I feel _____.
(Examples: amazed, impressed, small, happy)

Breathing in deeply, I can smell _____.
(Examples: the woods, salt water, earthy leaves, pine)

The colors I see are _____.

If I had discovered this place, I would have

named it _____.

TOP 5

What are the top five memories you have about your trip to this park?

1.

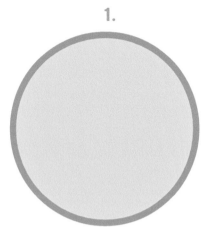

2.

3.

4.

5.

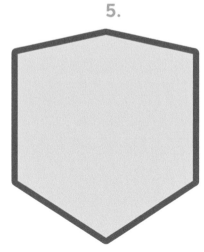

WHICH NATIONAL PARKS HAVE YOU VISITED?

Check off the U.S. national parks you have visited.

- ☐ Acadia
- ☐ Arches
- ☐ Badlands
- ☐ Big Bend
- ☐ Biscayne
- ☐ Black Canyon of the Gunnison
- ☐ Bryce Canyon
- ☐ Canyonlands
- ☐ Capitol Reef
- ☐ Carlsbad Caverns
- ☐ Channel Islands
- ☐ Congaree
- ☐ Crater Lake
- ☐ Cuyahoga Valley
- ☐ Death Valley
- ☐ Denali
- ☐ Dry Tortugas
- ☐ Everglades
- ☐ Gates of the Arctic
- ☐ Gateway Arch
- ☐ Glacier
- ☐ Glacier Bay

- ☐ Grand Canyon
- ☐ Grand Teton
- ☐ Great Basin
- ☐ Great Sand Dunes
- ☐ Great Smoky Mountains
- ☐ Guadalupe Mountains
- ☐ Haleakalā
- ☐ Hawai'i Volcanoes
- ☐ Hot Springs
- ☐ Indiana Dunes
- ☐ Isle Royale
- ☐ Joshua Tree
- ☐ Katmai
- ☐ Kenai Fjords
- ☐ Kings Canyon
- ☐ Kobuk Valley
- ☐ Lake Clark
- ☐ Lassen Volcanic
- ☐ Mammoth Cave
- ☐ Mesa Verde
- ☐ Mount Rainier

- ☐ National Park of American Samoa
- ☐ New River Gorge
- ☐ North Cascades
- ☐ Olympic
- ☐ Petrified Forest
- ☐ Pinnacles
- ☐ Redwood
- ☐ Rocky Mountain
- ☐ Saguaro
- ☐ Sequoia
- ☐ Shenandoah
- ☐ Theodore Roosevelt
- ☐ Virgin Islands
- ☐ Voyageurs
- ☐ White Sands
- ☐ Wind Cave
- ☐ Wrangell- St. Elias
- ☐ Yellowstone
- ☐ Yosemite
- ☐ Zion

EXPRESS YOURSELF

Use these pages to write notes or tape photos, tickets, or other paper souvenirs from your trip.

_____

_____

_____

_____

_____

_____

_____

_____

_____

_____

_____

_____

_____

_____

_____

_____

_____

_____

_____

_____

_____

_____

_____

_____

★ TRIP ★

TWO

_____
(Name of the national park you are visiting)

OFF TO THE PARK!

It's time to start tracking your adventure to a national park!

Date I'm leaving: _____

Who I'm going with: _____

Where I'm staying: _____

I'll be there for _____ **hours days weeks**
                      number   *(circle one)*

What I'm packing: _____

_____

_____

_____

What I wish I could pack: _____

_____

_____

_____

WHAT I KNOW ABOUT THIS NATIONAL PARK

This park is in the state of _____

It is near the city of _____

This park is known for_____

_____

This park should have: *(check all that apply)*

☐ A campground   ☐ Beaches

☐ Mountains   ☐ Tours

☐ A river   ☐ Caves

☐ A lake   ☐ Flowers

☐ Sand   ☐ Beautiful views of:

☐ Snow   ○ water

☐ Trails   ○ trees

☐ Trees   ○ open land

MY PLANS

The thing I'm most excited to do is: _____

_____

_____

The thing I can't wait to see is: _____

_____

_____

One thing I'm curious about is: _____

_____

_____

I hope the weather is: _____

_____

I hope the park has: _____

_____

_____

I hope I don't forget to: _____

_____

ARE WE THERE YET?

I'm traveling by: 🚗 ✈️ 🚆 🚲 ⛴️

The coolest thing I've seen out my window is:

_____

The weirdest thing I've seen out my window is:

_____

Travel snacks and meals I've had: _____

_____

Travel snacks and meals I've spilled: _____

_____

I am traveling _____ miles.

This **will   will not** be my first time at this park.
    (circle one)

The funniest thing that's happened so far is:

_____

_____

_____

WE'RE HERE!

Ah, we finally arrived.

(circle a bold word in each sentence)

My first impression was:
WOWZA!   **It's okay.**   **Yawn.**

It took **less** **more** time to get here than
I expected.

As soon as we got here, I **ate** **slept** **explored**
unpacked.

The first person I met was: _____

_____

Place your next steps in order from 1 to 5:

_____ Map out a hike

_____ Watch park film or talk to ranger

_____ Check weather forecast

_____ Fill water bottle

_____ Locate nearest bathroom

WOULD YOU RATHER . . .

Circle the choice you prefer.

* Hike wearing scuba flippers or high heels?

* Tour the park in a helicopter but be blindfolded or ride through it on a bicycle sitting backward?

* Be a park ranger answering questions or a tourist asking them?

* Have to spend the whole day wearing your pants inside out or wearing two different shoes?

* Sit in front of a person kicking your seat or sit in front of a crying baby?

* Be served garlic ice cream or dinner rolls filled with hot peppers?

* Be in this park in the summer but dressed for winter or in winter but dressed for summer?

THE PARK SO FAR

Things I've done so far: *(check all that apply)*

☐ Talked to a ranger

☐ Taken a picture at park entrance sign

☐ Went on a hike

☐ Walked through a museum

☐ Seen or heard an animal

☐ Had a snack or picnic

☐ Went on a scenic drive

☐ Had to put on a warmer jacket

☐ Got in the water

☐ Had fun!

I think this park is: *(check all that apply)*

☐ Big

☐ Small

☐ Quiet

☐ Loud

☐ Wild

☐ Historic

☐ Exciting

☐ Pretty

☐ A place I'd like to visit again

☐ Other _____

ANIMAL SIGHTINGS

The rangers need your help to study the behavior of the wildlife in the park. They need you to record what you observe about an animal. (If you haven't seen one yet, pick one that you learned about.)

What is your favorite animal that you've seen or

read about? _____

_____

What does it do during the day? _____

_____

What do you think it eats? _____

_____

Where do you think it sleeps? _____

_____

Draw the animal here:

PLANT POWER

Draw a life-size leaf from a tree or plant you find in the park. Make sure you don't damage a plant or take any leaves with you.

GETTING TO KNOW THE NATIONAL PARKS

Ready for more fun facts about the parks? Let's go!

* National parks are patrolled and protected by the rangers of the **National Park Service** (NPS). The National Park Service is part of the United States government.

* There are more than sixty main national parks and more than 400 other **national monuments**, seashores, historic sites, and battlefields.

* The logo of the NPS is in the shape of an arrowhead, which stands for history. On the arrowhead is a bison, which stands for wildlife. A tree, mountains, and a lake stand for the scenery.

* National Park Service rangers have worn green and gray **uniforms** for more than 100 years. Their flat hats protect them from the sun, rain, and snow.

THE BIG PICTURE

Draw your favorite feature of the park.

ROCK TALK

We can learn so much from rocks about how a place has changed over time. Most rocks were made millions of years ago. Find a rock to study. Make sure to leave it where it is.

Draw your rock:

What colors do you see in the rock?

☐ Black   ☐ Pink

☐ Blue   ☐ Red

☐ Brown   ☐ Sparkles

☐ Gray   ☐ White

☐ Green   ☐ Yellow

☐ Orange   ☐ Other _____

How does the rock feel?

☐ Smooth   ☐ Surprisingly light

☐ Sandy   ☐ Round

☐ Flat   ☐ Jagged

☐ Heavy   ☐ Other _____

HEY YOU, ANIMAL!

Ask a fellow traveler to help fill in the blanks.

Ranger _____ was hiking along the
person

_____ trail when she heard a _____
person _description_

sound. She thought it might be a(n) _____
animal

so she pressed her _____ to the lens of
body part

her binoculars to get a _____ look. She
description

was wrong; it was a _____ that was
different animal

digging through a pile of _____. "We can't
things

have that," she said. So, she took her best

_____ and banged it against a _____
thing _thing_

to get the animal's attention. It _____
action with -ed

off _____. The next day, she
description ending with -ly

came back to the pile to _____ it up, so that
action

no animal would ever want to _____ around
action

it again.

WISH YOU WERE HERE

Write a postcard to a friend or family member at home. What have you seen that you want to tell them about?

MAP A TRAIL

Map a trail you hiked or design a trail of your own! Draw the shape of your trail and use the map key to mark the things you might see. Add your own sights to the key.

Trail name: _____

Day and time hiked: _____

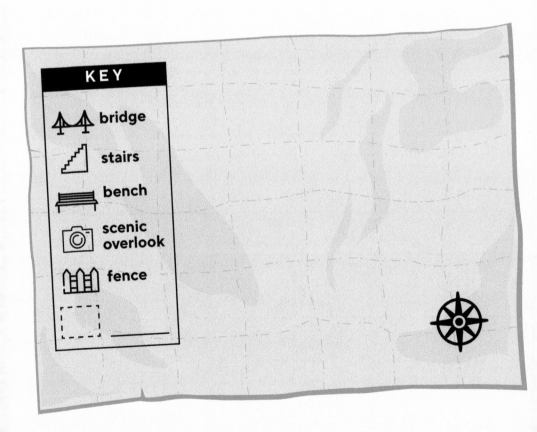

DEEP THOUGHTS

Find a quiet place to look at the scenery. Look around for a few minutes. Try to relax.

If you lived right here, what would your house look like? _____

_____

_____

_____

What do you think the first people who saw this place thought? _____

_____

_____

_____

How can we keep protecting this beautiful place? _____

_____

_____

_____

TOP 5

What are the top five
memories you have about
your trip to this park?

1.

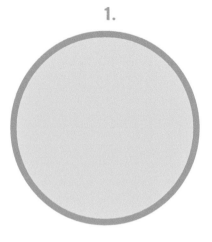

2.

3.

4.

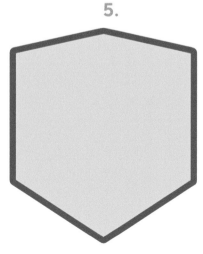

5.

GETTING TO KNOW THE NATIONAL PARKS

America's national parks are pretty extreme. Let's learn how:

* The hottest place on Earth is **Death Valley National Park**. It can get to more than 130 degrees Fahrenheit. That's hot enough to fry an egg!

* **Denali** is the highest mountain peak in North America. It grows an inch every twenty-four years! You can see it from 200 miles away.

* **Mammoth Cave** in Kentucky is the longest cave in the world. So far, more than 400 miles of the cave have been found.

* Yosemite Falls in **Yosemite National Park** is three waterfalls in one! It's also the tallest waterfall in North America.

* The **Grand Canyon** in Arizona is one mile deep, double the height of the tallest building in the world.

EXPRESS YOURSELF

Use these pages to write notes or tape photos, tickets, or other paper souvenirs from your trip.

_____

_____

_____

_____

_____

_____

_____

_____

_____

_____

_____

_____

_____

_____

_____

_____

_____

_____

_____

_____

_____

_____

_____

_____

_____

★ TRIP ★

THREE

_____
(Name of the national park you are visiting)

OFF TO THE PARK!

It's time to start tracking your adventure to a national park!

Date I'm leaving: _____

Who I'm going with: _____

Where I'm staying: _____

I'll be there for _____ **_hours days weeks_**
                          number   *(circle one)*

What I'm packing: _____

_____

_____

_____

What I wish I could pack: _____

_____

_____

_____

WHAT I KNOW ABOUT THIS NATIONAL PARK

This park is in the state of _____

It is near the city of _____

This park is known for _____

_____

This park should have: *(check all that apply)*

☐ A campground

☐ Mountains

☐ A river

☐ A lake

☐ Sand

☐ Snow

☐ Trails

☐ Trees

☐ Beaches

☐ Tours

☐ Caves

☐ Flowers

☐ Beautiful views of:

　○ water

　○ trees

　○ open land

MY PLANS

The thing I'm most excited to do is: _____

_____

_____

The thing I can't wait to see is: _____

_____

_____

One thing I'm curious about is: _____

_____

_____

I hope the weather is: _____

_____

I hope the park has: _____

_____

_____

I hope I don't forget to: _____

_____

ARE WE THERE YET?

I'm traveling by: 🚗 ✈️ 🚆 🚲 ⛴️

The coolest thing I've seen out my window is:

_____

The weirdest thing I've seen out my window is:

_____

Travel snacks and meals I've had: _____

_____

Travel snacks and meals I've spilled: _____

_____

I am traveling _____ miles.

This **will   will not** be my first time at this park.
(circle one)

The funniest thing that's happened so far is:

_____

_____

_____

WE'RE HERE!

Ah, we finally arrived.

(circle a bold word in each sentence)

My first impression was:
WOWZA!   It's okay.   Yawn.

It took **less   more**   time to get here than
I expected.

As soon as we got here, I **ate   slept   explored
unpacked**.

The first person I met was:_____

_____

Place your next steps in order from 1 to 5:

_____ Map out a hike

_____ Watch park film or talk to ranger

_____ Check weather forecast

_____ Fill water bottle

_____ Locate nearest bathroom

SOMEONE ELSE'S VIEW!

What does a fellow traveler think of the park? Ask them to tell you what they think and see and write it down below.

_____

_____

_____

_____

_____

_____

_____

_____

_____

_____

_____

THE PARK SO FAR

Things I've done so far: *(check all that apply)*

☐ Talked to a ranger

☐ Taken a picture at park entrance sign

☐ Went on a hike

☐ Walked through a museum

☐ Seen or heard an animal

☐ Had a snack or picnic

☐ Went on a scenic drive

☐ Had to put on a warmer jacket

☐ Got in the water

☐ Had fun!

I think this park is: *(check all that apply)*

☐ Big

☐ Small

☐ Quiet

☐ Loud

☐ Wild

☐ Historic

☐ Exciting

☐ Pretty

☐ A place I'd like to visit again

☐ Other _____

ANIMAL SIGHTINGS

The rangers need your help to study the behavior of the wildlife in the park. They need you to record what you observe about an animal. (If you haven't seen one yet, pick one that you learned about.)

What is your favorite animal that you've seen or read about? _____

_____

What does it do during the day? _____

_____

What do you think it eats? _____

_____

Where do you think it sleeps? _____

_____

Draw the animal here:

BE A PLANT DETECTIVE!

The rangers need you to help them observe plants in the park! Look for clues that help the plants survive.

Plant: _____

Where sighted: _____

Color: _____

Smell: _____

Have you ever seen it before? **Yes No**

I thought it was: ***beautiful   ugly   weird boring   cool***

Its overall plant shape looks like this:

GETTING TO KNOW THE NATIONAL PARKS

Trees are a big part of parks. Let's learn about a few!

* Sequoia trees are some of the world's largest living things. California's **Sequoia National Park** is home to the largest living tree in the world. It's 275 feet tall and 36 feet wide!

* The tallest tree in the world is another sequoia, this one in **Redwood National Park**. It's called the Hyperion Tree, and it is 379 feet tall! Its exact location is kept a secret to keep it safe.

* Bristlecone pine trees are found in **Great Basin National Park** in Nevada. They can live to be more than 5,000 years old! The oldest tree in the world is a Bristlecone pine, but its location is also kept secret.

* Joshua trees in **Joshua Tree National Park** actually aren't trees at all; they're members of the yucca family.

THE BIG PICTURE

Draw your favorite feature of the park.

SEEK AND FIND

Try to find these things in and around the park:

- ☐ Animal tracks
- ☐ Any animal you've never seen or heard before
- ☐ Bird in the air
- ☐ Bird on the ground
- ☐ Bugs
- ☐ Campers
- ☐ Drinking fountain
- ☐ Feather
- ☐ Fire ring
- ☐ Fish
- ☐ Park ranger

- ☐ Recycle bin
- ☐ Rock grouping
- ☐ Someone sneezing
- ☐ Squirrel
- ☐ Tall grass
- ☐ Tour bus
- ☐ Trail sign
- ☐ Tree smaller than you
- ☐ Tree taller than you
- ☐ Wooden stairs
- ☐ Worm
- ☐ "You are here" sign

The most unexpected thing I saw was:

_____

_____

LOST IN THE WOODS

Ask a fellow traveler to help fill in the blanks.

Mr. _____ was hiking through the
last name

_____ forest at _____ National
describing word   *name*

Park. After several _____ hours, he
number

found himself near the _____ geyser.
noun

The geyser _____ hot _____ from
action word   *thing*

the ground every _____ minutes. By
number

keeping the geyser in sight, he knew which

way he was _____ . He walked
action word with –ing

_____ toward the _____ and made
direction   *place*

sure he could still see the geyser. He found his

way back to the _____ , which was his first
thing

stop on his _____ . He could finally
action word

_____ back to the _____ and
action word   *place*

get a good night's rest.

WISH YOU WERE HERE

Write a postcard to a friend or family member at home. What have you seen that you want to tell them about?

MAP A TRAIL

Map a trail you hiked or design a trail of your own! Draw the shape of your trail and use the map key to mark the things you might see. Add your own sights to the key.

Trail name: _____

Day and time hiked: _____

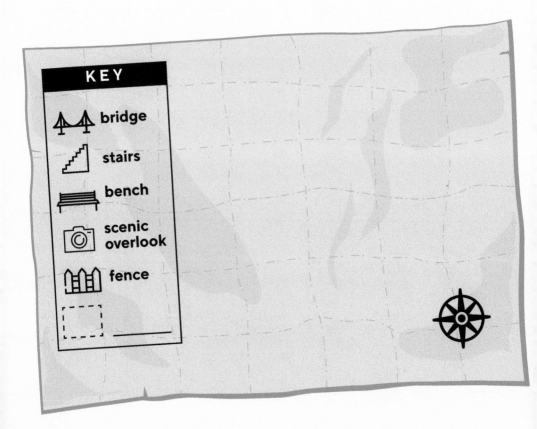

OBSERVE YOUR SURROUNDINGS

Fill this out when you get to a special place, such as a trailhead or a scenic overlook.

Location: _____

The ground feels _____.
(*Examples: hard, rough, smooth, grassy, wet*)

The air feels _____.
(*Examples: cold, sticky, breezy, warm, still*)

When I look around, I feel _____.
(*Examples: amazed, impressed, small, happy*)

Breathing in deeply, I can smell _____.
(*Examples: the woods, salt water, earthy leaves, pine*)

The colors I see are _____.

If I had discovered this place, I would have

named it _____.

TOP 5

What are the top five memories you have about your trip to this park?

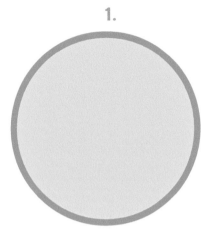

1.

2.

3.

4.

5.

GETTING TO KNOW THE NATIONAL PARKS

National parks are home to more than 400 different endangered animals. Let's learn about some of them!

* Grizzly bears are found in **Glacier, Grand Teton**, and **Yellowstone national parks**. They can weigh as much as 700 pounds. But they're still fast! They can run up to 40 miles per hour. In the winter, they hibernate—or sleep—for five to seven months.

* California condors once lived all over the western half of the United States, but by 1982, only twenty-two were alive. Condors are making a comeback thanks to their protection in national parks like **Pinnacles** and **Grand Canyon**. Some 500 live in the wild.

* Humpback whales are named so because they arch their backs before making a dive. They can travel up to 5,000 miles, often to **Glacier Bay National Park** in Alaska, to feed.

EXPRESS YOURSELF

Use these pages to write notes or tape photos, tickets, or other paper souvenirs from your trip.

_____

_____

_____

_____

_____

_____

_____

_____

_____

_____

★ · TRIP · ★

FOUR

(Name of the national park you are visiting)

OFF TO THE PARK!

It's time to start tracking your adventure to a national park!

Date I'm leaving: _____

Who I'm going with: _____

Where I'm staying: _____

I'll be there for _____ **hours days weeks**
              number   *(circle one)*

What I'm packing: _____

_____

_____

_____

What I wish I could pack: _____

_____

_____

_____

WHAT I KNOW ABOUT THIS NATIONAL PARK

This park is in the state of _____

It is near the city of _____

This park is known for _____

_____

This park should have: *(check all that apply)*

- ☐ A campground
- ☐ Mountains
- ☐ A river
- ☐ A lake
- ☐ Sand
- ☐ Snow
- ☐ Trails
- ☐ Trees

- ☐ Beaches
- ☐ Tours
- ☐ Caves
- ☐ Flowers
- ☐ Beautiful views of:
  - ○ water
  - ○ trees
  - ○ open land

MY PLANS

The thing I'm most excited to do is: _____

_____

_____

The thing I can't wait to see is: _____

_____

_____

One thing I'm curious about is: _____

_____

_____

I hope the weather is: _____

_____

I hope the park has: _____

_____

_____

I hope I don't forget to: _____

_____

ARE WE THERE YET?

I'm traveling by: 🚗 ✈️ 🚆 🚲 🛳️

The coolest thing I've seen out my window is:

_____

The weirdest thing I've seen out my window is:

_____

Travel snacks and meals I've had: _____

_____

Travel snacks and meals I've spilled: _____

_____

I am traveling _____ miles.

This **will** **will not** be my first time at this park.
(circle one)

The funniest thing that's happened so far is:

_____

_____

_____

WE'RE HERE!

Ah, we finally arrived.

(circle a bold word in each sentence)

My first impression was:
WOWZA!   It's okay.   Yawn.

It took   **less   more**   time to get here than
I expected.

As soon as we got here, I **ate   slept   explored
unpacked**.

The first person I met was:_____

_____

Place your next steps in order from 1 to 5:

_____ Map out a hike

_____ Watch park film or talk to ranger

_____ Check weather forecast

_____ Fill water bottle

_____ Locate nearest bathroom

THIS PARK NEEDS YOUR HELP!

If you could add some extra protection for the plants and animals in the park, what would you do? Add more fences? More trash cans? Place more rangers on patrol? What kind of new rules would you enforce?

_____

_____

_____

_____

_____

_____

_____

_____

_____

_____

THE PARK SO FAR

Things I've done so far: *(check all that apply)*

☐ Talked to a ranger

☐ Taken a picture at park entrance sign

☐ Went on a hike

☐ Walked through a museum

☐ Seen or heard an animal

☐ Had a snack or picnic

☐ Went on a scenic drive

☐ Had to put on a warmer jacket

☐ Got in the water

☐ Had fun!

I think this park is: *(check all that apply)*

☐ Big

☐ Small

☐ Quiet

☐ Loud

☐ Wild

☐ Historic

☐ Exciting

☐ Pretty

☐ A place I'd like to visit again

☐ Other _____

YOUR OWN ANIMAL

If you were to design the perfect animal for this park, what would it look like?

It would have _____ legs.

(circle a bold word in each sentence)
It would have **fur feathers scales skin**.

It would have **round teeth   sharp fangs a beak**.

It would eat _____ .

Draw your animal below.

PLANT POWER

Draw a life-size leaf from a tree or plant you find in the park. Make sure you don't damage a plant or take any leaves with you.

GETTING TO KNOW THE NATIONAL PARKS

Time to dive into some highs and lows of the parks!

* ★ **Gates of the Arctic National Park** in Alaska is the least-visited national park, with fewer than 8,000 people visiting each year.

* ★ **Great Smoky Mountains National Park** in Tennessee is the most visited, with more than fourteen million visitors per year!

* ★ Trail Ridge Road in **Rocky Mountain National Park** is the highest continually paved road in the United States.

* ★ **Petrified Forest National Park** in Arizona is one of the largest and most colorful places in the world to find petrified wood.

* ★ **Carlsbad Caverns National Park** in New Mexico has the country's deepest cave. It's 1,593 feet deep.

* ★ **Crater Lake National Park** in Oregon has the deepest lake in the United States. It's 1,943 feet deep.

THE BIG PICTURE

Draw your favorite feature of the park.

WOULD YOU RATHER . . .

Circle the choice you prefer.

★ Eat what the birds eat in this park or eat what the fish eat?

★ Spend the rest of your life in this park or never visit another park again?

★ Hike through a cave full of bats or canoe in a river full of alligators?

★ Go to a park with your friend's family or have your friend go to a park with your family?

★ Have pickles added to every meal or have mustard added to every meal?

★ Have someone else visit a beautiful park and describe it to you in detail or visit a beautiful park yourself but not get to describe it to anyone?

THE LIFE OF A BUG

Ask a fellow traveler to help fill in the blanks.

_____ the _____ and
name of a person on trip with you   type of bug

their _____ family was crawling along
        same bug

a _____ when they heard a loud
        thing

_____ . It was a great big _____
type of noise   color

_____ , who had just fallen off a
type of small animal

_____ log. The _____ was
describing word   same small animal

more than _____ feet tall and _____ ,
              number   emotion

so _____ screamed HIDE MY
        same person

_____! Heading away from the danger, they
snacks

ran right into a _____ _____ leaf.
                  describing word   same color

It was very _____-y but would protect
              kind of smell

them from all the wild _____ that
                        same animal

roamed the forest floor. The _____-y
                              same smell

leaf made a _____ home for
              describing word

them. They rode it like a speed boat until it

_____ on the shoreline.
action with -ed

WISH YOU WERE HERE

Write a postcard to a friend or family member at home. What have you seen that you want to tell them about?

MAP A TRAIL

Map a trail you hiked or design a trail of your own! Draw the shape of your trail and use the map key to mark the things you might see. Add your own sights to the key.

Trail name: _____

Day and time hiked: _____

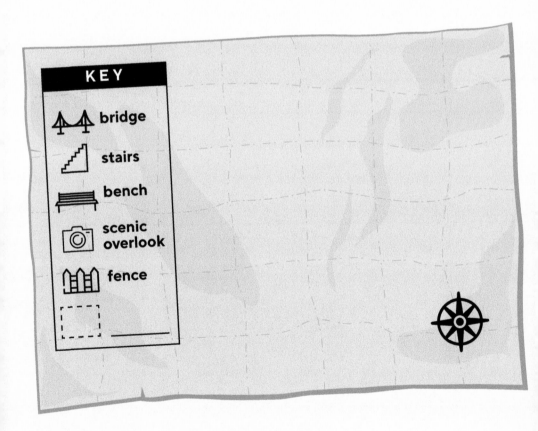

KEY

bridge

stairs

bench

scenic overlook

fence

WEATHER REPORT

How were the skies during your visit?

☐ Cloudy   ☐ Sunny

☐ Clear   ☐ Gray

☐ Overcast   ☐ Blue

How was the temperature?

☐ Cold   ☐ Mild

☐ Warm   ☐ All over the place!

☐ Hot

Was there any rain, wind, or snow?

☐ Yes   ☐ No

Were there drastic changes in temperature at night compared to morning?

☐ Yes   ☐ No

Draw the sky from where you're sitting right now. Are there clouds? Sun? Moon?

TOP 5

What are the top five memories you have about your trip to this park?

1.

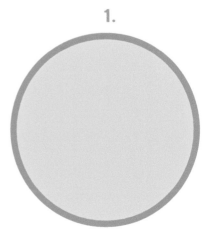

2.

3.

4.

5.

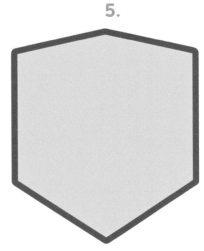

GETTING TO KNOW THE NATIONAL PARKS

Let's learn about life-forms—old and new—found in the parks!

★ Dinosaur bones have been found in many parks, such as **Petrified Forest** in Arizona, **Carlsbad Caverns** in New Mexico, and **Guadalupe Mountains** in Texas.

★ The oldest human footprints in North America were found in **White Sands National Park** in New Mexico. They are more than 21,000 years old.

★ In 2006, twenty-seven new species of insects were found in **Kings Canyon National Park**, including new kinds of spiders and centipedes.

★ A tiny fish called the Devils Hole pupfish was found in a pond of water inside a cavern at **Death Valley National Park**. The pond is the only place in the world where this fish lives.

EXPRESS YOURSELF

Use these pages to write notes or tape photos, tickets, or other paper souvenirs from your trip.

_____

_____

_____

_____

_____

_____

_____

_____

_____

_____

_____

ABOUT THE AUTHORS

 **Jason and Abby Epperson** have been traveling the United States full-time with their three boys since 2016. Their life on the road has led them to dozens of national parks, inspiring them to create the *America's National Parks Podcast* to share stories of these great places. You can find it at nationalparkpodcast. com or on any podcast app.